Congressional
Research
Service

Current Debates over Exchange Rates: Overview and Issues for Congress

Rebecca M. Nelson
Analyst in International Trade and Finance

November 12, 2013

Congressional Research Service

7-5700

www.crs.gov

R43242

Summary

Exchange rates are important in the international economy, because they affect the price of every country's imports and exports, as well as the value of every overseas investment. Following the global financial crisis of 2008-2009 and ensuing economic recession, disagreements among countries over exchange rates have become more widespread. Some policy leaders and analysts contend that there is a "currency war" now underway among certain countries.

At the heart of current disagreements is whether or not countries are using exchange rate policies to undermine free markets and intentionally push down the value of their currency in order to gain a trade advantage at the expense of other countries. A weak currency makes exports cheaper to foreigners, which can lead to higher exports and job creation in the export sector. However, if one country weakens its currency, there can be implications for other countries. In general, exporters and firms producing import-sensitive goods may find it harder to compete against countries with weak currencies. However, consumers and businesses that rely on inputs from abroad may benefit when other countries have weak currencies, because imports may become cheaper.

The United States has found itself on both sides of the current debates over exchange rates. On one hand, some Members of Congress and U.S. policy experts argue that U.S. exports and U.S. jobs have been adversely affected by the exchange rate policies adopted by China, Japan, and a number of other countries. On the other hand, some emerging markets, including Brazil and Russia, have argued that expansionary monetary policies in the United States and other developed countries caused the currencies of developed countries to depreciate, hurting the competitiveness of emerging markets. More recently, however, emerging-market currencies have started to depreciate, and now there are concerns about emerging-market currencies becoming too weak relative to the currencies of some developed economies.

Through the International Monetary Fund (IMF), countries have committed to avoid "currency manipulation." There are also provisions in U.S. law to address "currency manipulation" by other countries. In the context of recent disagreements, neither the IMF nor the U.S. Treasury Department has determined any country to be manipulating its exchange rate. There are differing views on why. Some argue that countries have not engaged in policies that violate international commitments on exchange rates or triggered provisions in U.S. law relating to currency manipulation. Others argue that currency manipulation has occurred, but that estimating a currency's "true" or "fundamental" value is complicated, and that the current international financial architecture is not effective at responding to exchange rate disputes.

Policy Options for Congress

Some Members of Congress may consider addressing exchange rate issues because they are concerned about the impact of other countries' exchange rate policies on the competitiveness of U.S. products. Recently, concerns have been raised about the impact of Japan's economic policies on the value of the yen, and the implications for the U.S. economy. However, there are a number of potential consequences from taking action on exchange rates that Congress might also want to consider. For example, U.S. imports from countries with weak currencies may be less expensive than they would be otherwise; countries may retaliate after being labeled a currency "manipulator"; and tensions over exchange rates could dissipate as the global economy strengthens.

If Members did decide to take action, they have a number of options for doing so. Options could include urging the Administration to address currency disputes at the IMF and in trade agreements, or passing legislation relating to countries determined to have undervalued exchange rates, among others. Two bills have been introduced in the 113th Congress related to exchange rate policies in other countries (H.R. 1276; S. 1114). Representative Levin has also released a proposal for addressing currency issues in the Trans-Pacific Partnership, a proposed free trade agreement that the United States is negotiating with Japan and 10 other Asia-Pacific countries.

Contents

Figures

Contacts

Introduction

Some policy makers and analysts allege that certain countries are using exchange rate policies to gain an "unfair" trade advantage. They maintain that some countries are purposefully using various policies to weaken the value of their currency to boost exports and create jobs, but that these policies come at the expense of other countries. Some political leaders and policy experts contend that there is a "currency war" in the global economy, as countries compete against each other to weaken the value of their currencies and boost exports.[1]

The United States has found itself on both sides of the debate. On one hand, some Members of Congress and U.S. policy experts argue that U.S. producers and U.S. jobs have been adversely affected by the exchange rate policies adopted by China, Japan, and a number of other countries. On the other hand, some emerging markets, including Brazil and Russia, have argued that expansionary monetary policies in the United States and other major developed countries have reduced the value of the dollar and other currencies, and thereby have hurt the competitiveness of emerging markets. More recently, some in the United States have started discussing pulling back expansionary monetary policies, and emerging-market currencies have started to weaken. There are now concerns about emerging-market currencies becoming too weak relative to the currencies of some developed economies.

During the 113th Congress, some Members of Congress have proposed taking action on exchange rate issues:

- Legislation has been introduced aimed at countries determined to have fundamentally undervalued or misaligned exchange rates (the Currency Reform for Fair Trade Act, H.R. 1276; the Currency Exchange Rate Oversight Reform Act of 2013, S. 1114).

- Some Members have expressed concerns about Japan's monetary policies and its effect on exchange rates, which impact the competitiveness of U.S. exports. These concerns have been raised particularly in the context of the Trans-Pacific Partnership (TPP) negotiations. TPP is a proposed regional trade agreement that the United States is negotiating with Japan and 10 other countries in the Asia-Pacific region.[2] In June 2013, 230 Representatives sent a letter to President Obama urging the Administration to address unfair exchange rate policies in the TPP, particularly with regards to Japan.[3] In September 2013, 60 Senators sent a letter to the Treasury Secretary, Jacob Lew, and the U.S. Trade Representative, Michael Froman, asking them to address currency "manipulation" in the TPP and

---

[1] For example, see "Brazil Warns of World Currency War," *Reuters*, September 28, 2010; Fred Bergsten, "Currency Wars, the Economy of the United States, and Reform of the International Monetary System," Remarks at Peterson Institute for International Economics, May 16, 2013, http://www.iie.com/publications/papers/bergsten201305.pdf.

[2] For more information on TPP, see CRS Report R42694, *The Trans-Pacific Partnership Negotiations and Issues for Congress*, coordinated by Ian F. Fergusson.

[3] Representative Mike Michaud, "Majority of House Members Push Obama to Address Currency Manipulation in TPP," Press Release, June 6, 2013, http://michaud.house.gov/press-release/majority-house-members-push-obama-address-currency-manipulation-tpp.

all future free trade agreements.[4] Representative Levin released a specific proposal to address unfair exchange rate practices in the TPP in July 2013.[5]

- Some Members have also called on the Administration to address currency issues in negotiations with the European Union (EU) over a proposed free trade agreement (the Transatlantic Trade and Investment Partnership [TTIP]) and in renewal of Trade Promotion Authority (TPA).[6] TPA is the authority Congress grants to the President to enter into certain reciprocal trade agreements and to have their implementing bills considered under expedited legislative procedures when certain conditions have been met.[7] TPA expired in 2007 and some Members are looking to renew it to facilitate trade negotiations.

This report provides information on current debates over exchange rates in the global economy. It offers an overview of how exchange rates work; analyzes specific disagreements and debates; and examines existing frameworks for potentially addressing currency disputes. It also lays out some policy options available to Congress, should Members want to take action on exchange rate issues.

The Importance of Exchange Rates in the Global Economy

What is an Exchange Rate?

An exchange rate is the price of a country's currency relative to other currencies. In other words, it is the rate at which one currency can be converted into another currency. For example, on August 30, 2013, one U.S. dollar could be exchanged for 0.76 euros (€), 98 Japanese yen (¥), or 0.65 British pounds (£).[8] Exchange rates are expressed in terms of dollars per foreign currency, or expressed in terms of foreign currency per dollar. The exchange rate between dollars and euros on August 30, 2013, can be quoted as 1.32 $/€ or, equivalently, 0.76 €/$.

---

[4] Senator Debbie Stabenow, "Sixty Senators Urge Administration to Crack Down on Currency Manipulation in Trans-Pacific Partnership Talks," Press Release, September 24, 2013, http://www.stabenow.senate.gov/?p=press_release&id=1171. The U.S. auto industry in particular has been supportive of efforts to address currency manipulation in TPP. For example, see Michael Stumo, "American Auto Industry Applauds Senate Currency Letter," *Trade Reform*, September 25, 2013.

[5] U.S. Representative Sander Levin, "U.S.-Japan Automotive Trade: Proposal to Level the Playing Field," http://www.piie.com/publications/papers/levin20130723proposal.pdf.

[6] For example, see U.S. Congress, House Ways and Means, *U.S. Trade Representative Michael Froman*, 113th Cong., 1st sess., July 18, 2013; U.S. Congress, Senate Finance, *Confirmation Hearing on the Nomination of Michael Froman to be U.S. Trade Representative*, 113th Cong., 1st sess., June 6, 2013. For more on TTIP, see CRS Report R43158, *Proposed Transatlantic Trade and Investment Partnership (TTIP): In Brief*, by Shayerah Ilias Akhtar and Vivian C. Jones. For more information about TPA, see CRS Report RL33743, *Trade Promotion Authority (TPA) and the Role of Congress in Trade Policy*, by J. F. Hornbeck and William H. Cooper.

[7] For more on TPA, see CRS Report RL33743, *Trade Promotion Authority (TPA) and the Role of Congress in Trade Policy*, by J. F. Hornbeck and William H. Cooper.

[8] Exchange rate data in this report is from the Federal Reserve, unless otherwise noted.

Consumers use exchange rates to calculate the cost of goods produced in other countries. For example, U.S. consumers use exchange rates to calculate how much a bottle of French or Australian wine costs in U.S. dollars. Likewise, French and Australian consumers use exchange rates to calculate how much a bottle of U.S. wine costs in euros or Australian dollars.

How much a currency is worth in relation to another currency is determined by the supply and demand for currencies in the foreign exchange market (the market in which foreign currencies are traded). The foreign exchange market is substantial, and has expanded in recent years. Trading in foreign exchange markets averaged $5.3 trillion per day in April 2013, up from $3.3 trillion in April 2007.[9]

The relative demand for currencies reflects the underlying demand for goods and assets denominated in that currency, and large international capital flows can have a strong influence on the demand for various currencies. The government, typically the central bank, can use policies to shape the supply of its currency in international capital markets.

Different Measures of Exchange Rates

- **Nominal vs. real exchange rate:** The nominal exchange rate is the rate at which two currencies can be exchanged, or how much one currency is worth in terms of another currency. The real exchange rate measures the value of a country's goods against those of another country at the prevailing nominal exchange rate. Essentially, the real exchange rate adjusts the nominal exchange rate for differences in prices (and rates of inflation) across countries.

- **Bilateral vs. effective exchange rate:** The bilateral exchange rate is the value of one currency in terms of another currency. The effective exchange rate is the value of a currency against a weighted average of several currencies (a "basket" of foreign currencies). The basket can be weighted in different ways, such as by share of world trade or GDP. The Bank for International Settlements (BIS), for example, publishes data on effective exchange rates.[10]

Impact on International Trade and Investment

International Trade

Exchange rates affect the price of every export leaving a country and every import entering a country. As a result, changes in the exchange rate can impact trade flows. When the value of a country's currency falls, or depreciates, relative to another currency, its exports become less expensive to foreigners and imports from overseas become more expensive to domestic consumers.[11] These changes in relative prices can cause the level of exports to rise and the level of imports to fall.[12] For example, if the dollar depreciates against the British pound, U.S. exports

---

[9] Bank for International Settlements, "Foreign Exchange Turnover in April 2013: Preliminary Global Results," *Triennial Central Bank Survey*, September 2013, https://www.bis.org/publ/rpfx13fx.pdf.

[10] For example, see "BIS Effective Exchange Rate Indices," http://www.bis.org/statistics/eer/.

[11] This assumes that changes in the exchange rate are reflected in retail and consumer prices. In practice, there may be factors that limit the "pass through" of changes in the exchange rates to changes in prices. For example, contracts may lock in prices of imports and exports for a set amount of time.

[12] It may take time for changes in the exchange rate to result in changes in the volume of tradable goods and services. For example, if imports become more expensive, it may take time for domestic consumers to find suitable domestic or foreign substitutes.

become cheaper to UK consumers, and imports from the UK become more expensive to U.S. consumers. As a result, U.S. exports to the UK may rise, and U.S. imports from the UK may fall.

Likewise, when the value of a currency rises, or appreciates, the country's exports become more expensive to foreigners and imports become less expensive to domestic consumers. This can cause exports to fall and imports to rise. For example, if the dollar appreciates against the Australian dollar, U.S. exports become more expensive to Australian consumers, and imports from Australia become less expensive to U.S. consumers. Changes in prices may cause U.S. exports to Australia to fall and U.S. imports from Australia to rise.

International Investment

Exchange rates impact international investment in two ways. First, exchange rates determine the value of existing overseas investments. When a currency depreciates, the value of investments denominated in that currency falls for overseas investors. Likewise, when a currency appreciates, the value of investments denominated in that currency rises for overseas investors. For example, if a U.S. investor holds a German government bond denominated in euros, and the euro depreciates, the value of the bond in U.S. dollars falls, making the investment worth less to the U.S. investor. In contrast, if the euro appreciates, the value of the German bond in U.S. dollars rises, and the investment is worth more to the U.S. investor.

Second, exchange rates impact the flow of investment across borders. Changes in the value of a currency today can shape investors' future expectations about the value of the currency, which can have substantial impacts on capital flows. If investors expect a currency to depreciate, overseas investors may be reluctant to invest in assets denominated in that currency and may want to sell assets denominated in the currency, in fear that their investments will become less valuable over time. Likewise, if a currency is expected to rise over time, assets denominated in that currency become more attractive to overseas investors. For example, a depreciating euro may deter U.S. investment in the Eurozone, while an appreciating euro may increase U.S. investment in the Eurozone.[13]

Types of Exchange Rate Policies

There are two major ways that the price of a country's currency is determined, or types of "currency regimes." First, some governments "float" their currencies. This means they allow the price of their currency to fluctuate depending on supply and demand for currencies in foreign exchange markets. Governments with floating exchange rates do not take policy actions to influence the value of their currencies.

Second, some countries "fix" or "peg" their exchange rate. This means they fix the value of their currency to another currency (such as the U.S. dollar or euro), a group (or "basket") of currencies, or a commodity, such as gold. The government (typically the central bank) then uses various policies to control the supply and demand for the currency in foreign exchange markets to

---

[13] The Eurozone refers to the 17 European Union (EU) member states that use the euro as their currency: Austria, Belgium, Cyprus, Estonia, Finland, France, Germany, Greece, Ireland, Italy, Luxembourg, Malta, the Netherlands, Portugal, Slovakia, Spain, and Slovenia. The other 10 EU members have yet to adopt the euro or have chosen not to adopt the euro.

maintain the set price for the currency. Often, central banks maintain exchange rate pegs by buying and selling currency in foreign exchange markets, or "intervening" in foreign exchange markets.

There are pros and cons to having a floating or fixed exchange rate. Fixed exchange rates provide more certainty in international transactions, but they can make it more difficult for the economy to adjust to economic shocks and can make the currency more susceptible to speculative attacks. Floating exchange rates introduce more unpredictability in international transactions and may deter international trade and investment, but make it easier for the economy to adjust to changes in economic conditions.

In order to take advantage of the benefits of both fixed and floating exchange rates, many countries do not adopt a purely fixed or floating exchange rate, but choose a hybrid policy: they let the currency's value fluctuate but take action to keep the exchange rate from deviating too far from a target value or zone. The degree to which they float or peg varies. The optimal choice for any given country will depend on its characteristics, including its size and interconnectedness to the country to which it would peg its currency.

Between the end of World War II and the early 1970s, most countries, including the United States, had fixed exchange rates.[14] In the early 1970s, when international capital flows increased, the United States abandoned its peg to gold and floated the dollar. Other countries' currencies were pegged to the dollar, and after the dollar floated, some other countries decided to float their currencies as well.

In 2012, 35% of countries had floating currencies.[15] This includes several major currencies, such as the U.S. dollar, the euro, the Japanese yen, and the British pound, whose economies together account for 50% of global GDP.[16] Many countries use policies to manage the value of their currencies, although some manage it more than others. This includes many small countries, such as Panama and Hong Kong, as well as a few larger economies, such as China, Russia, and Saudi Arabia. In 2012, 40% of countries used a "soft" peg, which let the exchange rate fluctuate within a desired range, and 13% of countries used a "hard" peg, which anchors the currency's value more strictly, including the formal adoption of a foreign currency to use as a domestic currency (for example, Ecuador has adopted the U.S. dollar as its national currency).[17] No large country uses a hard peg. **Figure 1** depicts the exchange rate policies adopted by different countries.

---

[14] Exchange rates were, in theory, fixed but "adjustable," meaning that countries could adjust their exchange rates to correct a "fundamental disequilibrium" in their exchange rate. In practice, it was rare for a country to adjust its exchange rate outside of a narrow band.

[15] IMF, "Annual Report on Exchange Arrangements and Exchange Restrictions," 2012, http://www.imf.org/external/pubs/nft/2012/eaer/ar2012.pdf. Exchange rate data on how the exchange rate policies work in practice (the "*de facto*" exchange rate policy), which may or may not match the official description of the policy (the "*de jure*" exchange rate policy). Countries that are members of a currency union (where multiple countries may adopt use of the same currency, including the Eurozone, the East Caribbean Currency Union, the West African Economic and Monetary Union, and the Central African Economic Community) are coded according to how the currency is managed. For example, the euro is a floating currency, and individual members of the Eurozone for this purpose are counted as having adopted floating exchange rates.

[16] IMF, *World Economic Outlook Database*, April 2013.

[17] 13% use other managed arrangements that do not fall neatly into a "soft" peg or "hard" peg category, sometimes because the government changes exchange rate policies frequently.

Figure 1. Map of Exchange Rate Policies by Country

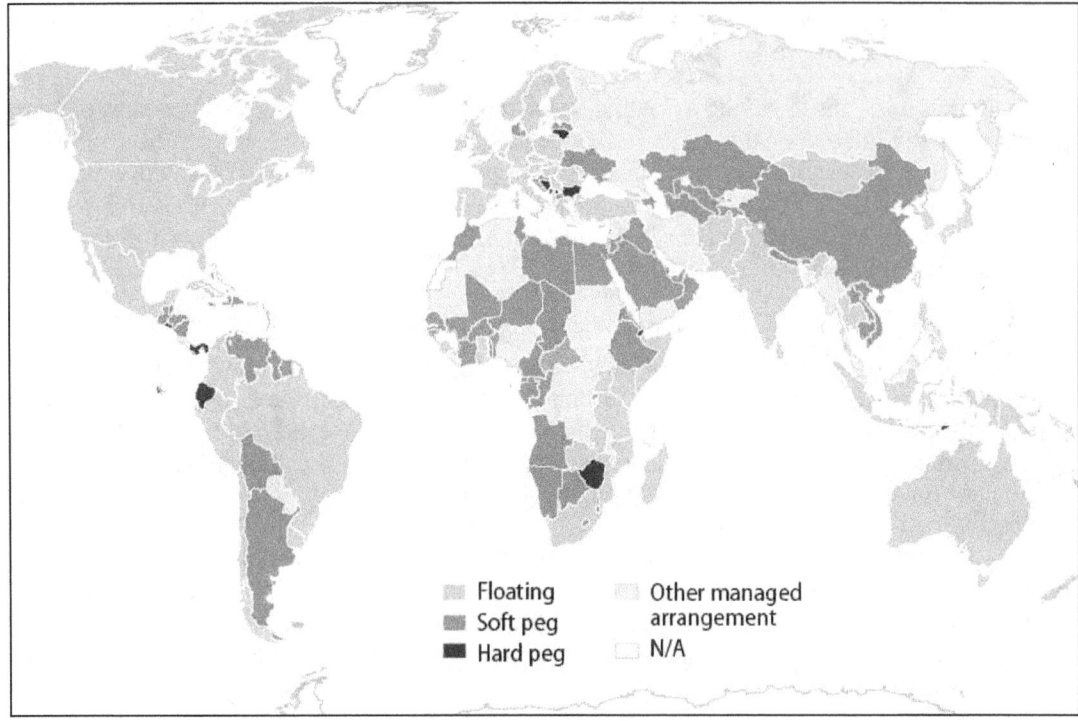

Source: IMF, "Annual Report on Exchange Arrangements and Exchange Restrictions," 2012.

Notes: See footnote 15.

Exchange Rate Misalignments

Many economists believe that exchange rate levels can differ from the underlying "fundamental" or "equilibrium" value of the exchange rate. When an actual exchange rate differs from its fundamental or equilibrium value, the currency is said to be misaligned. More specifically, when the actual exchange rate is too high, the currency is said to be overvalued; when the actual rate is too low, the currency is said to be undervalued.

Considerable debate exists about what the fundamental or equilibrium value of a currency is and how to define or calculate currency misalignment.[18] For example, some economists believe that a currency is misaligned when the exchange rate set by the government, or the official rate, differs from what would be set by the market if the currency were allowed to float. By this reasoning, governments that take policy actions to sustain an exchange rate peg, such as intervening in currency markets, most likely have misaligned currencies. Additionally, this view suggests that floating currencies, by definition, cannot be misaligned, since their values are determined by market forces.

---

[18] For example, see Enzo Cassino and David Oxley, "Exchange Rate Valuation and its Impact on the Real Economy," New Zealand Treasury, March 2013,
http://www rbnz.govt nz/research_and_publications/seminars_and_workshops/mar2013/5200821.pdf; Rebecca L. Driver and Peter F. Westaway, " Concepts of Equilibrium Exchange Rates," Bank of England, Working Paper No. 248, 2004, http://www.bankofengland.co.uk/publications/Documents/workingpapers/wp248.pdf.

For other economists, a currency can be misaligned even if it is a floating rate. This is the case if the exchange rate differs from its long-term equilibrium value, which is based on economic fundamentals and eliminates short-term factors that can cause the exchange rate to fluctuate. Defining or estimating an equilibrium exchange rate is not a straightforward process and is complex. Economists disagree on the factors that determine an equilibrium exchange rate, and whether the concept is a valid one, particularly when applied to countries with floating exchange rates. Economists have developed a number of models for calculating differences between actual exchange rates and equilibrium exchange rates. Estimates of whether a currency is misaligned, and if so, by how much, can vary widely depending on the model used.[19]

General Debates over "Currency Wars"

Amid heightened concerns about slow growth and high unemployment in many countries, disagreements over exchange rate policies have broadened after the global financial crisis. In 2010, Brazil's finance minister, Guido Mantega, declared that a "currency war" had broken out in the global economy.[20]

At the heart of current disagreements is whether or not countries are using policies to intentionally push down the value of their currency in order to gain a trade advantage at the expense of other countries. A weak currency makes exports cheaper to foreigners and imports more expensive to domestic consumers. This can lead to higher production of exports and import-competing goods, which could help spur export-led growth and job creation in the export sector.

However, if one country weakens its currency, there can be negative implications for certain sectors in other countries. In general, a weaker currency in one country can hurt exporters in other countries, since their exports become relatively more expensive and may fall as a result. Additionally, domestic firms producing import-competing goods may find it harder to compete with imports from countries with weak currencies, since weak currencies lower the cost of imports. Under certain circumstances, policies used to drive down the value of a currency in one country can cause other countries to run persistent trade deficits (imports exceed exports) that can be difficult to adjust and can be associated with the build-up of debt.

For these reasons, some economists view efforts to boost exports through a weaker exchange rate as "unfair" to other countries and a type of "beggar-thy-neighbor" policy—the benefit the country gets from the policy comes at the expense of other countries. These views are particularly rooted in the experience in the 1930s, during which, some economists argue, countries devalued their currencies to boost exports, in response to widespread high unemployment and negative economic conditions.[21] The devaluations in the 1930s are referred to as "competitive

---

[19] For example, see "Misleading Misalignments," *Economist*, June 21, 2007; Peter Isard, "Equilibrium Exchange Rates: Assessment Methodologies," IMF Working Paper WP/07/296, December 2007, http://www.imf.org/external/pubs/ft/wp/2007/wp07296.pdf; Treasury Department, "Semiannual Report on International Economic and Exchange Rate Policies," December 2006, Appendix 2, Exchange Rate Misalignment: What the Models Tell Us and Methodological Considerations," http://www.treasury.gov/resource-center/international/exchange-rate-policies/Documents/2006_Appendix-2.pdf.

[20] For example, see "Brazil Warns of World Currency War," *Reuters*, September 28, 2010.

[21] For example, see Beth A. Simmons, *Who Adjusts? Domestic Sources of Foreign Economic Policy During the Interwar Years.* (Princeton, NJ: Princeton University Press, 1994). Not all economists characterize changes in exchange rates during the 1930s as competitive devaluations. For example, some argue that countries were forced to devalue (continued...)

---

devaluations," since a devaluation in one country was often offset by a devaluation in another country, making it difficult for any country to gain a lasting advantage.[22] Some economists view the competitive devaluations of the 1930s as detrimental to international trade, and, in addition to protectionist trade policies, as exacerbating the Great Depression.

Many economists disagree that "currency wars" and competitive devaluations are currently underway in the global economy and argue that, if they are, they are not necessarily bad for the global economy. Because currency devaluations can often involve printing domestic currency, or implementing expansionary monetary policies, they can stimulate short-term economic growth.[23] If enough countries engage in currency interventions, then there may be no net change in relative exchange rate levels and the simultaneous currency interventions may help reflate the global economy and boost global economic growth. Economists of this viewpoint argue that competitive devaluations of the 1930s did not cause the Great Depression and, in fact, actually helped end it.[24]

Additionally, a weak currency in one country does not have an unambiguous negative effect on other countries. Instead, consumers and certain sectors may benefit when other countries have weak currencies. In particular, consumers that purchase imports from abroad benefit when other countries have weak currencies, because imports become cheaper. Additionally, businesses that rely on inputs from overseas also benefit when other countries have weak currencies, by lowering the costs of inputs and thus the overall cost of production.

Specific Debates over Exchange Rates

In current debates about exchange rates and whether countries are engaged in unfair currency policies to weaken their currencies, two major types of concerns have been raised: first, concerns about countries engaged in interventions in foreign currency markets, and second, concerns about the effects of expansionary monetary policies in some developed countries on exchange rate levels.

Currency Interventions

Governments have various mechanisms they can use to weaken, or devalue, their currency, or sustain a lower exchange rate than would exist in the absence of government intervention. One way is intervening in foreign exchange markets or, more specifically, selling domestic currency in exchange for foreign currency. These interventions increase the supply of domestic currency relative to other currencies in foreign exchange markets, pushing the price of the currency down. The foreign currency is typically then invested in foreign assets, most commonly government bonds.

(...continued)

because they were running out of gold reserves. See Douglas A. Irwin, *Trade Policy Disaster: Lessons from the 1930s* (Cambridge, MA: MIT Press, 2012).

[22] Depreciation is typically used to refer to a currency weakening due to market forces. When a government undertakes specific policies to weaken the value of its currency, it is typically referred to as a devaluation.

[23] For example, see Matthew O'Brien, "Currency Wars, What Are They Good For? Absolutely Ending Depressions," *The Atlantic*, February 5, 2013.

[24] Barry Eichengreen, "Currency War or International Policy Coordination?," University of California, Berkeley, January 2013, http://emlab.berkeley.edu/~eichengr/curr_war_JPM_2013.pdf.

Concerns about currency interventions are not new. For nearly a decade, various policy makers and analysts have raised concerns about China's interventions in foreign exchange markets to maintain, in their view, an undervalued currency relative to the U.S. dollar. Since the global financial crisis, however, concerns about currency interventions have become more widespread, as more countries, including Switzerland and others, have intervened in foreign exchange markets, in the view of some analysts, to lower the value of their currency.[25]

China[26]

Over the past decade, the Chinese government has tightly managed the value of its currency, the renminbi (RMB) or yuan, against the U.S. dollar.[27] Some policy makers and analysts believe that China's currency policies keep the RMB undervalued relative to the U.S. dollar. They argue that China's policies give Chinese exports an "unfair" trade advantage against U.S. exports and are a major contributing factor to the U.S. trade deficit with China.

In 1994, China began to peg its currency to the U.S. dollar and kept it pegged to the U.S. dollar at a constant rate through 2005. In July 2005, it moved to a managed peg system, in which the government allowed the currency to fluctuate within a range, and the currency began to appreciate. In 2008, China halted appreciation of the RMB, due to concerns about the effects of the global financial crisis on Chinese exports. In 2012, China again allowed more flexibility in the value of the RMB against the U.S. dollar. Between 2005 and the end of 2012, the RMB appreciated by almost 25% against the dollar (**Figure 2**).[28]

The Chinese government has used various policies, including intervening in foreign currency markets and capital controls, to manage this appreciation of the RMB against the U.S. dollar. It does so primarily by printing yuan and selling it for U.S. currency and assets denominated in U.S. dollars, usually U.S. government bonds. It also manages the value of its exchange rate through capital controls that limit buying and selling of RMB.[29] As China has engaged in currency interventions, its holdings of foreign exchange reserves have increased, from $715 billion in the first quarter of 2005 to $3,463 billion in the first quarter of 2013 (**Figure 2**), equivalent to about 38% of China's GDP.[30] Some economists view the sustained, substantial increase in foreign exchange reserves as evidence that the Chinese government keeps the value of the RMB below what it would be if the RMB were allowed to float freely.

More recently, some economists are starting to question whether the yuan is still undervalued against the U.S. dollar when adjusting for differences in price levels (the real exchange rate), and

---

[25] For example, see Alan Beattie, "Hostilities Escalate to Hidden Currency War," *Financial Times*, September 27, 2010.

[26] For more on China's currency, see CRS Report RL32165, *China's Currency: Economic Issues and Options for U.S. Trade Policy*, by Wayne M. Morrison and Marc Labonte.

[27] The official name of China's currency is the renminbi (RMB), which is denominated in yuan units. Both RMB and yuan are used interchangeably to refer to China's currency.

[28] Change in the nominal exchange rate (not adjusted for differences in inflation between China and the United States).

[29] The RMB is largely convertible on a current account (trade) basis, but not on a capital account basis, meaning that foreign exchange in China is not regularly obtainable for investment purposes. In other words, it can be difficult to purchase investments denominated in RMB.

[30] IMF, *International Financial Statistics*, 2013; IMF, *World Economic Outlook*, April 2013.

if so, by how much, particularly as inflation has increased in China.[31] They point to the fact that foreign exchange reserves have not grown as quickly since 2011 as some evidence of this adjustment. In July 2012, the IMF changed its assessment of the RMB's value from significantly undervalued to moderately undervalued.[32]

Figure 2. China's Exchange Rate and Foreign Exchange Reserves

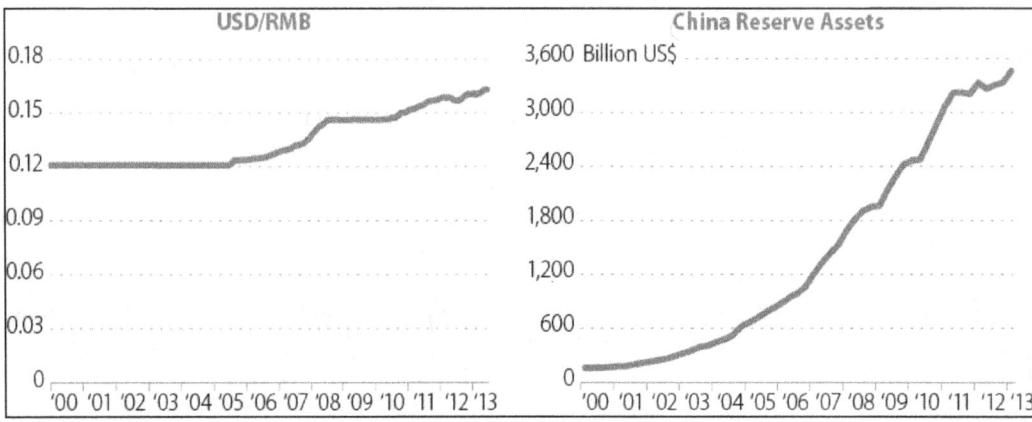

Source: Federal Reserve; IMF, *International Financial Statistics*.

Note: For the graph on the left, an increase represents an appreciation of the RMB relative to the U.S. dollar.

Switzerland

Before the global financial crisis of 2008-2009, Switzerland had a floating exchange rate. During the crisis, the Swiss franc was viewed as a "safe haven" currency, or a currency that investors trusted more than others and would therefore buy in times of uncertainty.[33] Increased investor demand for the Swiss franc put upward pressure on the currency, which, in turn, raised concerns for the Swiss government about the competitiveness of Swiss exports. In 2009 and 2010, the Swiss central bank (the National Bank of Switzerland) intervened in foreign exchange markets to prevent or limit appreciation of the Swiss franc against the euro, by selling Swiss francs for foreign currencies.[34] When a worsening of the Eurozone crisis put additional upward pressure on the Swiss franc, the Swiss central bank announced in September 2011 that it would buy "unlimited quantities" of foreign currency to keep the Swiss franc from appreciating above a specific value (**Figure 3**).[35] As a result of its currency interventions, Switzerland's foreign exchange reserves increased more than tenfold, from $46 billion in the fourth quarter of 2008 to

---

[31] "The Cheapest Thing Going is Gone," *Economist*, June 15, 2013.

[32] IMF, "IMF Executive Board Concludes 2012 Article IV Consultation with People's Republic of China," Public Information Notice No. 12/86, July 24, 2012, http://www.imf.org/external/np/sec/pn/2012/pn1286.htm; Simon Rabinovitch, "IMF Says Renminbi 'Moderately Undervalued'," *Financial Times*, July 25, 2012.

[33] Michael Bordo, Owen F. Humpage, Anna J. Schwartz, "Foreign-Exchange Intervention and the Fundamental Trilemma of International Finance: Notes for Currency Wars," *VoxEU*, June 18, 2012, http://www.voxeu.org/article/notes-currency-wars-trilemma-international-finance.

[34] U.S. Department of the Treasury, Office of International Affairs, "Report to Congress on International Economic and Exchange Rate Policies," July 8, 2010, http://www.treasury.gov/resource-center/international/exchange-rate-policies/Documents/Foreign%20Exchange%20Report%20July%202010.pdf.

[35] Swiss National Bank Press Release, September 6, 2011, http://www.snb.ch/en/mmr/reference/pre_20110906/source/pre_20110906.en.pdf.

$470 billion in the first quarter of 2013 (**Figure 3**), about 73% of Swiss GDP.[36] Before the financial crisis, the Swiss central bank had last intervened in the foreign exchange market in 1995.[37]

Many economists argue that the recent interventions by the Swiss central bank have held the value of the Swiss franc lower than it would be otherwise (if the currency floated freely and the Swiss central bank did not intervene in foreign exchange markets). They argue that this has given Swiss exports an advantage, helping Switzerland maintain a trade surplus and one of the lowest unemployment rates in Europe.[38] However, some economists have noted that Switzerland's trading partners have generally not "kicked up much fuss" over its interventions, and that Switzerland's interventions are the "overlooked" currency war in Europe.[39] This could be due to the small size of the Swiss economy, and a perception held by some that Swiss interventions are a defensive measure against developments in the rest of Europe that are beyond its control.

Figure 3. Switzerland's Exchange Rate and Foreign Exchange Reserves

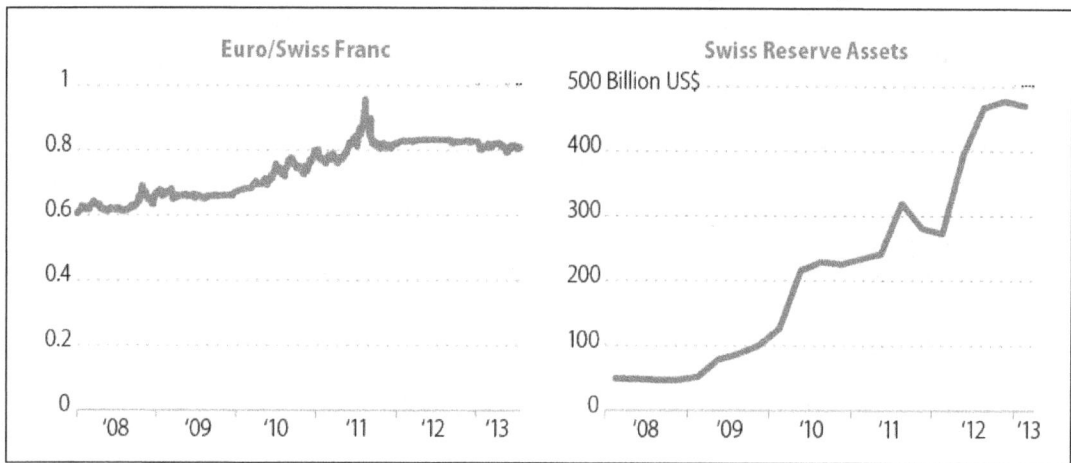

Source. European Central Bank; IMF, *International Financial Statistics.*

Note: For the graph on the left, an increase represents an appreciation of the Swiss franc relative to the euro.

Other Countries

Other examples of interventions to weaken currencies since the global financial crisis include, among others:

- **Japan,** which sold yen in foreign exchange markets in 2010 and 2011. Japan's interventions in March 2011 were unusual in that they were supported with corresponding interventions by the other G-7 countries to weaken the yen. A

---

[36] IMF, *International Financial Statistics*, 2013; IMF, *World Economic Outlook*, April 2013.

[37] Michael Bordo, Owen F. Humpage, Anna J. Schwartz, "Foreign-Exchange Intervention and the Fundamental Trilemma of International Finance: Notes for Currency Wars," *VoxEU*, June 18, 2012, http://www.voxeu.org/article/notes-currency-wars-trilemma-international-finance.

[38] Daniel Gros, "An Overlooked Currency War in Europe," *VoxEU*, October 11, 2012, http://www.voxeu.org/article/overlooked-currency-war-europe.

[39] Ibid., "Positive-Sum Currency Wars," *Economist*, February 14, 2013.

---

crisis in Japan (earthquake, tsunami, and threat of nuclear crisis) in March 2011 had sparked a sharp appreciation of the yen, which some feared would throw the world's third-largest economy back into recession, prompting the coordinated interventions;[40]

- **South Korea**, which is believed to have intervened in currency markets intermittently to hold down the value of the won in the latter part of 2012 and early 2013;[41] and

- **New Zealand**, whose central bank revealed in May 2013 that it had intervened in currency markets to stem appreciation of its currency, the New Zealand dollar (nicknamed the kiwi).[42]

More generally, according to a December 2012 study by the Peterson Institute of International Economics (PIIE), more than 20 countries have cumulatively increased their foreign exchange reserves by nearly $1 trillion annually for several years, mainly through interventions in foreign currency markets, and as a result have been able to keep their currencies "substantially undervalued."[43] The study identifies China, Denmark, Hong Kong, South Korea, Malaysia, Singapore, Switzerland, and Taiwan as most heavily engaged in currency interventions.

Debates

A number of countries are actively intervening, or have recently intervened, in foreign exchange markets to lower the value of their currencies, and there are different views among economists about the consequences of these interventions for other countries. Some economists argue that currency interventions have helped countries give their exports a boost at the expense of other countries. The December 2012 study by the PIIE estimates that currency interventions have caused the U.S. trade deficit to increase by $200 billion to $500 billion per year and the U.S. economy to lose between 1 million and 5 million jobs.[44] The study also argues that currency interventions have adversely affected the economies of Australia, Brazil, Canada, the Eurozone, India, and Mexico, in addition to a number of other developing economies.

Other economists are skeptical that one country's interventions in foreign exchange markets have had adverse consequences for other countries. For example, some economists argue that interventions in foreign exchange markets by other countries change the composition of output in

---

[40] Peter Garnham and David Oakley, "G7 Nations Co-ordinate $25bn Yen Sell-Off," *Financial Times*, March 18, 2011.

[41] According to the April 2013 Treasury report on exchange rates, the Korean government does not publish intervention data, but many market participants believe that the Korean authorities intervened in currency markets in the latter part of 2012 and early 2013. See U.S. Department of the Treasury, Office of International Affairs, "Report to Congress on International Economic and Exchange Rate Policies," April 12, 2013, http://www.treasury.gov/resource-center/international/exchange-rate-policies/Documents/Foreign%20Exchange%20Report%20April%202013.pdf.

[42] Alan Beattie, "Hostilities Escalate to Hidden Currency War," *Financial Times*, September 27, 2010; U.S. Department of the Treasury, Office of International Affairs, "Report to Congress on International Economic and Exchange Rate Policies," April 12, 2013, http://www.treasury.gov/resource-center/international/exchange-rate-policies/Documents/Foreign%20Exchange%20Report%20April%202013.pdf; Rebecca Howard, "NZ Central Bank Admits Currency Intervention to Dampen Dollar," *Dow Jones*, May 9, 2013.

[43] C. Fred Bergsten and Joseph E. Gagnon, "Currency Manipulation, the US Economy, and the Global Economic Order," Peterson Institute for International Economics Policy Brief 12-25, December 2012, http://www.iie.com/publications/interstitial.cfm?ResearchID=2302.

[44] Ibid.

---

the United States (particularly the size of the export and domestic-oriented sectors), but do not reduce the overall employment or output levels in the U.S. economy. Some economists also question whether currency interventions have long-lasting effects on exchange rate levels, particularly for countries with floating currencies. They argue that the large size of international capital flows overwhelms, in the long term, government purchases and sales of foreign currencies, and that other economic fundamentals, such as interest rates, inflation rates, and overall economic performance, have much greater effects on exchange rate levels.

Still other economists argue that it is hard to make generalizations about the effects of currency interventions, and that, depending on the specific circumstances, currency interventions may or may not be "fair" policies.[45] For example, they argue that relevant factors can include:

- **Does the government intervene in currency markets to sometimes strengthen and sometimes weaken its currency, or does it always intervene to weaken its currency?** "Two-way" interventions (sometimes strengthening the currency, sometimes weakening the currency) may be evidence that the country is using currency interventions to sustain a pegged exchange rate that is close to its long-term fundamental or equilibrium value. Some economists argue that "one-way" interventions (always selling domestic currency) may be evidence that the government is using interventions to sustain a currency that is below the currency's fundamental or equilibrium value.

- **Does the government intervene periodically, or on a continual basis?** Periodic interventions may smooth potentially disruptive short-term fluctuations in the exchange rate and help the country build foreign exchange reserves, which can help it guard against economic crises. Sustained, or long-term, interventions may create negative distortions in the global economy.

- **Does the government allow the intervention to increase its domestic money supply, or does the government "sterilize" the intervention to prevent an increase in its domestic money supply?** When some governments intervene in currency markets by selling domestic currency, they allow the domestic money supply to increase. This is called an unsterilized intervention. When other countries (such as China and, sometimes, Switzerland) intervene, they do not allow their money supply to increase. Instead, when they sell domestic currency in exchange for foreign currency, they then sell a corresponding quantity of domestic government bonds to remove the extra domestic currency from circulation. This is called a sterilized intervention. It may matter to other countries whether the intervening country sterilizes the intervention or not. For example, increasing the money supply may help increase domestic demand, which in certain circumstances can cause consumers to buy more, not fewer, imports from other countries. Additionally, an increase in the money supply may cause prices to rise in the medium term. This may mean that the exchange rate adjusted for inflation (the real exchange rate) may not change in the medium term (after prices adjust), even if the nominal exchange rate (the exchange rate not adjusted for inflation) falls.

---

[45] For example, see Matthew O'Brien, "Currency Wars, What Are They Good For? Absolutely Ending Depressions," *The Atlantic*, February 5, 2013; "Trial of Strength," *Economist*, September 23, 2010.

Expansionary Monetary Policies

In addition to intervening directly in foreign exchange markets, governments can weaken the value of their currency through expansionary monetary policies. Monetary policy is the process by which a government (usually the central bank) controls the supply of money in an economy, such as by changing the interest rates through buying and selling government bonds. Changes in the money supply can impact the value of the currency. For example, increasing the supply of British pounds can cause the price of the pound to fall.

Some emerging markets, particularly Brazil, have been critical of the expansionary monetary policies adopted by the United States, the United Kingdom, and the Eurozone in response to the global financial crisis of 2008-2009. A number of countries have also raised concerns about Japan's monetary policies, following a major policy shift in late 2012 and early 2013.

Quantitative Easing in the United States, UK, and Eurozone[46]

The United States, the United Kingdom, and, to a lesser extent, the Eurozone adopted expansionary monetary policies to respond to the economic recession following the global financial crisis of 2008-2009. In addition to cutting interest rates, the Federal Reserve, the Bank of England, and the European Central Bank (ECB) used quantitative easing to provide further monetary stimulus. Quantitative easing is an unconventional form of monetary policy that expands the money supply through government purchases of assets, usually government bonds. Quantitative easing is typically used when more conventional monetary policy tools are no longer feasible, for example, when short-term interest rates cannot be cut because they are already near zero.

Some emerging markets have argued that because the U.S. dollar, the British pound, and the euro are floating currencies, expansionary policies in these countries have caused these currencies to depreciate against the currencies of emerging markets. For example, Brazil has argued that quantitative easing in developed countries was a key factor in causing its currency (the real) to appreciate by more than 25% against the dollar between the start of 2009 and the end of the third quarter of 2010 (see **Figure 4**), when Brazil's finance minister, Guido Mantega, declared that a currency "war" had broken out in the global economy.[47] Brazil imposed some short-term controls on inflows of capital into Brazil (capital controls) to stem appreciation of the real.[48]

In response to the concerns of emerging markets, many policy makers and analysts have argued that the Federal Reserve, the Bank of England, and the ECB adopted expansionary monetary policies for domestic purposes (combatting the recession), and that any effect on their currencies was a side-effect or by-product of the policy.[49] For example, during a Senate Banking Committee hearing in February 2013, the Chairman of the Federal Reserve, Ben Bernanke, stressed that the Federal Reserve is not engaged in a currency war or targeting the value of the U.S. dollar.[50]

---

[46] For more on quantitative easing in the United States, see CRS Report R42962, *Federal Reserve: Unconventional Monetary Policy Options*, by Marc Labonte.

[47] For example, see "Brazil Warns of World Currency War," *Reuters*, September 28, 2010. In this report, exchange rate data is from the Federal Reserve unless otherwise noted.

[48] Samantha Pearson, "Brazil Launches Fresh 'Currency War' Offensive," *Financial Times*, March 15, 2012.

[49] For example, see "Phoney Currency Wars," *Economist*, February 16, 2013.

[50] U.S. Congress, Senate Banking, Housing, and Urban Affairs, *Hearing on the Semi-Annual Monetary Policy Report*, (continued...)

Instead, he emphasized that monetary policy is being used to achieve domestic economic objectives (high employment and price stability). He also stressed that monetary policies to strengthen aggregate demand in the United States are not "zero-sum," because they raise the demand for the exports of other countries.

The concerns of emerging markets about the effects of quantitative easing have eased in recent months. As developed countries have started discussing rolling back expansionary monetary policies, the real has weakened substantially against the U.S. dollar (see **Figure 4**). Brazil's government, in fact, has started expressing concerns about the real becoming too weak, and in August 2013, intervened in foreign currency markets to strengthen its currency.[51] The concerns of emerging-market economies about the potential rollback of quantitative easing policies in developed countries, including the United States, were a major topic of discussion at the September 2013 G-20 summit in St. Petersburg, Russia.[52]

Figure 4. U.S. Dollar-Brazilian Real Exchange Rate

Source: Federal Reserve.

Note: An increase represents an appreciation of the Brazilian real relative to the U.S. dollar.

Japan and "Abenomics"

Concerns have also been recently raised about major changes in Japan's monetary policy and their effects on the value of the yen. Elected in December 2012, Prime Minister Shinzo Abe has made it a priority of his administration to grow Japan's economy and eliminate deflation (falling prices), which has plagued Japan for many years. His economic plan, nicknamed "Abenomics," relies on three major economic policies: expansionary monetary policies, fiscal stimulus, and structural reforms. To promote expansionary monetary policy, Japan's central bank (the Bank of

---

(...continued)

113th Cong., 1st sess., February 26, 2013.

[51] For example, see Matthew Malinowski and Blake Schmidt, "Brazil Real Surges on $60 Billion Intervention Plan," *Bloomberg*, August 23, 2013.

[52] G-20 Leaders' Declaration, September 2013, St. Petersburg, http://www.g20.org/documents.

Japan) unveiled a host of new measures in the first half of 2013, including goals to double the monetary base (commercial bank reserves plus currency circulating in the public) and to double its holdings of Japanese government bonds. By buying government bonds in exchange for yen, the Bank of Japan can increase Japan's money supply.

Changes in Japan's monetary policies, along with fiscal stimulus measures, appear to be contributing to a strengthening of Japan's economy. For example, in July 2013, the IMF upgraded its forecast of growth in Japan for 2013, from 1.5% to 2.0%.[53] However, the expansionary monetary policies may have also contributed to a relatively sharp depreciation of the yen, which fell more than 25% between mid-2012 and mid-2013 (see **Figure 5**), even as Japan has not directly intervened in currency markets since 2011.

Several countries have expressed their concerns about a weakening of the yen. An official from the Russian central bank reportedly warned that "Japan is weakening the yen and other countries may follow," and that "the world is on the brink of a fresh currency war."[54] Additionally, the president of China's sovereign wealth fund reportedly warned Japan against using its neighbors as a "garbage bin" by deliberately devaluing the yen, and South Korea's finance minister argued that Japan's weakening yen hurts his country's economy more than threats from North Korea.[55] Movements in Japan's currency have also created concerns for some Members of Congress, with concerns being raised about the currency policies in the context of the TPP, where Japan is one of the negotiating parties.

Others argue that a weakening yen in recent months has partially offset the slow, but continued, appreciation of the yen in the preceding several years (**Figure 5**). For example, in January 2012, the IMF estimated that the Japanese yen was "moderately overvalued from a medium-term perspective."[56] Some also argue that, rather than targeting the value of the currency, Japan's monetary policies are targeting domestic objectives, namely, beating deflation that has plagued the economy for many years. Japan's finance minister, Taro Aso, reportedly stated that "monetary easing is aimed at pulling Japan out of deflation quickly. It is not accurate at all to criticize (us) for manipulating currencies."[57]

---

[53] IMF, *World Economic Outlook Update*, July 9, 2013, http://www.imf.org/external/pubs/ft/weo/2013/update/02/.

[54] Simon Kennedy and Scott Rose, "Russia Says World is Nearing Currency War as Europe Joins," *Bloomberg*, January 16, 2013.

[55] Lingling Wei, "China Fund Warns Japan Against a 'Currency War,'" *Wall Street Journal*, March 6, 2013; Cynthia Kim, "South Korea's Hyun Says Yen Bigger Issue than North Korea," *Bloomberg*, April 18, 2013.

[56] IMF, "Japan: Solid Recovery, but Europe Dampens Outlook," IMF Survey Online, June 12, 2012, http://www.imf.org/external/pubs/ft/survey/so/2012/car061112b htm.

[57] "Japan Denies Currency Manipulation Claims Ahead of G20," *Reuters*, January 25, 2013.

Figure 5. U.S. Dollar-Japanese Yen Exchange Rate

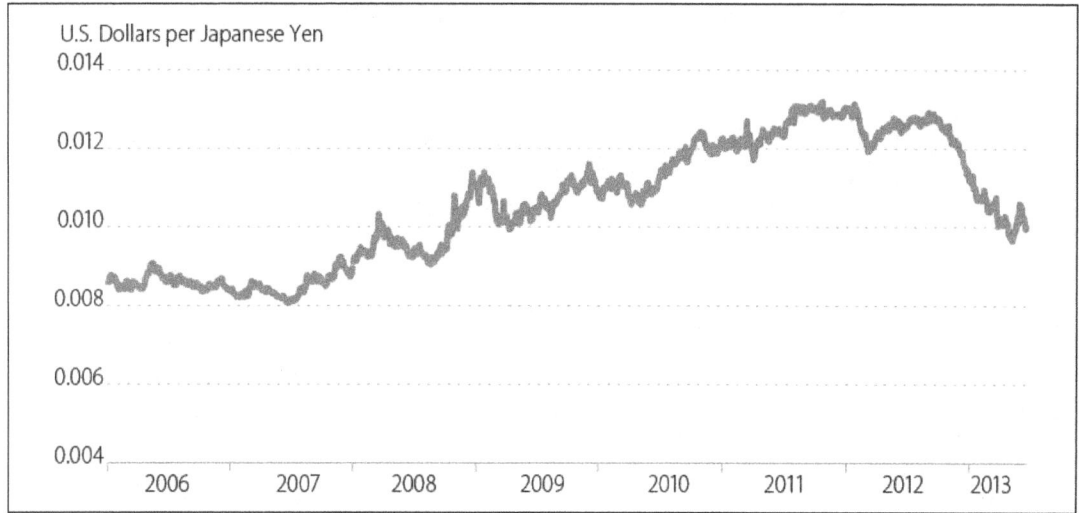

Source: Federal Reserve.

Note: A decrease represents a depreciation of the yen relative to the U.S. dollar.

Debates

There is debate over whether the expansionary monetary policies, including quantitative easing, implemented by some developed economies have been "beggar-thy-neighbor" policies. Some argue that expansionary monetary policies have unfairly caused the currencies of developed countries to depreciate against other countries, giving the exports of developed countries an "unfair" export boost. However, most economists agree that the expansionary policies in the United States, the UK, the Eurozone, and Japan have been designed to stimulate their domestic economies and will, in the medium term, cause prices to rise. As a result, they argue that there will be little effect on the real exchange rate (the exchange rate adjusted for differences in prices across countries) in the medium term (as prices increase), even if the nominal exchange rate (the exchange rate not adjusted for differences in prices across countries) falls in the short term. However, it should be noted that inflation in all these countries remains very low, to date.

Additionally, some argue that the expansionary policies stimulate domestic consumption and investment, which ordinarily leads to higher, not lower, imports from other countries, all else being equal.[58] They argue that the net effect of quantitative easing and similar policies on trading partners is not necessarily negative and could be positive in some instances. For example, the IMF estimated that the first round of quantitative easing in the United States resulted in substantial output gains for the rest of the world, and that the second round generated modest output gains for the rest of the world.[59]

For some economists, then, a key question to evaluate whether expansionary monetary policies are "fair" or "unfair" in the context of claims about "currency wars" is:

---

[58] "Positive-Sum Currency Wars," *Economist*, February 14, 2013.

[59] IMF, "The United States Spillover Report – 2011 Article IV Consultation," IMF Country Report No. 11/203, July 2011, pp. 32, http://www.imf.org/external/pubs/ft/scr/2011/cr11203.pdf.

- **Is it appropriate for countries to adopt expansionary monetary policies to combat a domestic economic recession, even if some sectors in other countries may be adversely affected in the short run?:** Some economists argue that it is entirely "natural" for countries to unilaterally adopt the monetary policies to suit their specific needs of the domestic economy, and that countries should use expansionary monetary policies to respond to economic recessions.[60] Moreover, most central banks, including the Fed, are pursuing statutory mandates that do not include foreign exchange rate requirements and responsibilities. Other economists argue that countries have a number of policy tools to respond to economic recessions, not just monetary policy, and that in today's globalized economy, a country should consider the potential negative spillover effects on other countries in its decision-making process.

Addressing Disagreements over Exchange Rates

Government policies that impact exchange rates have been a source of contention among countries. Various avenues have been developed or explored over the years to address specific currency disputes, both at the multilateral level and through U.S. law, with varying degrees of impact.

On the multilateral front, countries have made commitments to refrain from "manipulating" their exchange rates to gain an unfair trade advantage through the International Monetary Fund (IMF). Additionally, some argue that commitments made in the context of the World Trade Organization (WTO) are relevant to disagreements over exchange rates, although this view is disputed. Exchange rate issues have also been addressed in the past through less formal channels of international economic coordination among small groups of developed economies.

In addition to these multilateral forums, the United States has also adopted legislation to address unfair exchange rate policies pursued by other countries. In 1988, Congress enacted legislation to address "currency manipulation" by other countries. Congress has also included provisions on exchange rates in previous TPA legislation.

Exchange rate issues have been a key source of discussion at recent G-7 and G-20 meetings, but little formal or concrete action has occurred beyond these discussions.[61] Neither the IMF nor the U.S. Treasury Department has found any country to be manipulating its exchange rate in recent years.

---

[60] For example, see Jeffrey Frankel, "Dispatches from the Currency Wars," *Project Syndicate*, June 11, 2013. http://www.project-syndicate.org/blog/dispatches-from-the-currency-wars.

[61] The Group of 7 (G-7) includes Canada, France, Germany, Italy, Japan, the United States, and the United Kingdom. The Group of 20 (G-20) includes the G-7 countries plus Argentina, Australia, Brazil, Canada, China, India, Indonesia, Mexico, Russia, Saudi Arabia, South Africa, South Korea, Turkey, and the European Union (EU). For more on the G-20, see CRS Report R40977, *The G-20 and International Economic Cooperation: Background and Implications for Congress*, by Rebecca M. Nelson.

Forums to Potentially Address Disagreements

International Monetary Fund

With a nearly universal membership of 188 countries, the IMF is focused on promoting international monetary stability.[62] The IMF has engaged on the exchange rate policies of its member countries as part of its mandate, arguably motivated by the experience of competitive devaluations in the 1930s.[63] Its role on exchange rates has evolved over time.[64] Currently, IMF member countries have agreed to several obligations on exchange rates in the IMF's Articles of Agreement, the document that lays out the rules governing the IMF and establishes a "code of conduct" for IMF member countries.[65] The Articles state that countries can use whatever exchange rate system they wish—fixed or floating—so long as they follow certain guidelines; that countries should seek, in their foreign exchange and monetary policies, to promote orderly economic growth and financial stability; and that the IMF should engage in "firm" surveillance over the exchange rate policies of its members.[66]

The Articles also state that IMF member countries are to "avoid manipulating exchange rates or the international monetary system in order to prevent effective balance of payments adjustment or to gain an unfair advantage over other members."[67] An IMF Decision, issued in 1977 and updated in 2007 and 2012, provides further guidance that, among other things, "a member will only be considered to be manipulating exchange rates in order to gain an unfair competitive advantage over other members if the Fund determines both that: (a) the member is engaged in these policies for the purposes of securing fundamental exchange rate misalignment in the form of an undervalued exchange rate; and (b) the purpose of securing such misalignment is to increase net exports."[68]

---

[62] For more on the IMF, CRS Report R42019, *International Monetary Fund: Background and Issues for Congress*, by Martin A. Weiss.

[63] For example, see Morris Goldstein, "Currency Manipulation and Enforcing the Rules of the International Monetary System," in *Reforming the IMF for the 21st Century*, ed. Edwin M. Truman, Special Report 19 ed. (Institute for International Economics, 2006), http://www.piie.com/publications/chapters_preview/3870/05iie3870.pdf.

[64] Between the end of World War II and the early 1970s, the IMF supervised a fixed exchange rate system, in which the value of all currencies was fixed to the U.S. dollar, and the value of the dollar was fixed to gold. Countries could not change their exchange rates by more than 10% without the Fund's consent, and could only do so to correct a "fundamental disequilibrium" in exchange rate values. This system broke down in the early 1970s when the United States floated its currency, and some other countries subsequently decided to float their currencies as well. After a period of turmoil in world currency markets, an amendment to the IMF's founding document—the Articles of Agreement—was adopted in 1978. This Amendment laid out member countries' obligations on exchange rate policies to incorporate the shift to floating currencies adopted by some IMF member countries.

[65] IMF Articles of Agreement (as amended), http://www.imf.org/External/Pubs/FT/AA/#art4.

[66] IMF Article IV.

[67] Effective balance of payments adjustment generally refers to a country's ability to, over time, balance its international transactions, particularly relating to the capital account (financial transactions) and its current account (export and import of goods and services, plus income and other unilateral transfers, such as gifts or remittances).

[68] IMF, "IMF Executive Board Adopts New Decision on Bilateral Surveillance over Members' Policies," Public Information Notice (PIN) No. 07/69, June 21, 2007, http://www.imf.org/external/np/sec/pn/2007/pn0769.htm; IMF, "IMF Executive Board Adopts New Decision on Bilateral and Multilateral Surveillance," Public Information Notice (PIN) No. 12/89, July 30, 2012, http://www.imf.org/external/np/sec/pn/2012/pn1289.htm.

If a member country were to be found to be in violation of its obligations to the IMF, under the rules laid out in the Articles, it could be punished through restrictions on its access to IMF funding, suspension of its voting rights at the IMF, or, ultimately, expulsion from the IMF.[69]

To date, the IMF has never publicly labeled a member country a currency manipulator.[70] Some argue that the IMF's definition of currency "manipulation" has made it tough to go after currency "manipulators." They argue that it requires the IMF to determine or demonstrate that policies shaping the exchange rate level have been for the express purpose of increasing net exports, and that "intent" is hard to establish.[71] Even if the IMF could demonstrate a country is manipulating its exchange rate under its definition of the term, some analysts also argue that, in practice, the IMF does not have a credible mechanism for dealing with "manipulators," particularly countries that are not reliant on IMF financing.[72] They argue that it is extremely unlikely the IMF would actually strip violators of their IMF voting rights or expel them from the institution.

World Trade Organization

With 159 member countries, the WTO is the principal international organization governing world trade. It was established in 1995 as a successor institution to the General Agreement on Tariffs and Trade (GATT), a post-World War II institution intended to liberalize and promote nondiscrimination in trade among countries. Unique among the major international trade and finance organizations, the WTO has a mechanism for enforcing its rules through a dispute settlement process.

Given the relationship between exchange rates and trade, some have argued that the World Trade Organization (WTO) has a role to play in responding to currency disputes. Some analysts and lawyers have examined whether WTO provisions allow for recourse against countries that are unfairly undervaluing its currency.[73]

One aspect of the debate is whether WTO agreement on export subsidies applies to countries with undervalued currencies. The WTO Agreement on Subsidies and Countervailing Measures specifies that countries may not provide subsidies to help promote their national exports, and countries are entitled to levy countervailing duties on imported products that receive subsidies from their national government.[74] Some economists maintain that an undervalued currency lowers a firm's cost of production relative to world prices and therefore helps encourage exports. Some argue, then, that an undervalued currency should count as an export subsidy. It is not clear, however, whether intentional undervaluation of a country's currency is an export subsidy under

---

[69] IMF Articles of Agreement, Article XXVI:2.

[70] Joseph E. Gagnon, "Combating Widespread Currency Manipulation," Peterson Institute for International Economics Policy Brief PB12-19, July 2012, http://www.iie.com/publications/pb/pb12-19.pdf.

[71] Claus D. Zimmermann, "Exchange Rate Misalignment and International Law," *The American Journal of International Law*, vol. 105, no. 3 (July 2011), pp. 423-476.

[72] Ibid.

[73] For example, see Robert W. Staiger and Alan O. Sykes, "'Currency Manipulation' and World Trade," *World Trade Review*, vol. 9, no. 4 (2010), pp. 583-627; Haneul Jung, "Tackling Currency Manipulation with International Law: Why and How Currency Manipulation Should be Adjudicated?," *Manchester Journal of International Economic Law*, vol. 9, no. 2 (2012), pp. 184-200.

[74] WTO Agreement on Subsidies and Countervailing Measures, http://www.wto.org/english/docs_e/legal_e/24-scm.pdf.

---

the WTO's specific definition of the term, and thus is eligible for recourse through countervailing duties under WTO agreements. For example, the subsidy must be, among other things, specific to an industry and not provided generally to all producers. There is debate over whether intentional undervaluation of a currency is "industry specific" because it applies to everyone.

Another aspect of the debate relates to a provision in the GATT (the WTO agreement on international trade in goods), which states that member countries "shall not, by exchange action, frustrate intent of the provisions" of the agreement.[75] Some analysts argue that policies to undervalue a currency are protectionist policies, and thus should count as an exchange rate action that frustrates the intent of the GATT. Others argue that the language is too vague to apply to undervalued currencies.[76] Specifically, they argue that the language was written to apply to an international system of exchange rates that no longer exists (the system of fixed exchange rates, combined with capital controls, that prevailed from the end of World War II to the early 1970s).

No dispute over exchange rates has been brought before the WTO,[77] and whether currency disputes fall under the WTO's jurisdiction remains a contested issue.[78]

Less Formal Multilateral Coordination: The G-7 and the G-20

In addition to formal international institutions focused on economic issues, like the IMF and the WTO, countries also use less formal forums to coordinate economic policies. Before the global financial crisis of 2008-2009, the primary forum was a small group of seven advanced economies, the G-7.[79] Following the crisis, the G-20, a larger group of advanced and emerging-market countries, became the premier forum for international economic coordination.[80]

In the past, small groups of advanced economies had had more success in addressing currency issues through this type of less formal international cooperation. For example, in 1985, France, West Germany, Japan, the United States, and the UK signed the Plaza Accord, in which countries agreed to intervene in currency markets to depreciate the U.S. dollar in relation to the Japanese yen and the German deutsche mark to address the U.S. trade deficit. In 1987, six countries (the five signatories of the Plaza Accord, plus Canada) signed the Louvre Accord, in which they

---

[75] GATT Article XV(4), http://www.wto.org/english/docs_e/legal_e/gatt47_01_e htm#articleXV.

[76] For example, see Aaditya Mattoo and Arvind Subramanian, "Currency Undervaluation and Sovereign Wealth Funds: A New Role for the World Trade Organization," Peterson Institute for International Economics Working Paper WP 08-2, January 2008, http://www.petersoninstitute.org/publications/wp/wp08-2.pdf; Gary Hufbauer, Yee Wong, and Ketki Sheth, *US-China Trade Disputes: Rising Tide, Rising Stakes*. Policy Analyses in International Economics 78. Washington: Institute for International Economics, 2006; Michael Waibel, "Retaliating Against Exchange-Rate Manipulation under WTO Rules," *VoxEU*, April 16, 2010, http://www.voxeu.org/article/retaliating-against-exchange-rate-manipulation-under-wto-rules.

[77] Robert E. Scott, "Currency Manipulation—History Shows that Sanctions are Needed," Economic Policy Institute, April 29, 2010, http://www.epi.org/publication/pm164/.

[78] Gregory Hudson, Pedro Bento de Faria, and Tobias Peyerl, "The Legality of Exchange Rate Undervaluation Under WTO Law," Geneva Graduate Institute, Center for Trade and Economic Integration Working Paper, July 2011, http://graduateinstitute.ch/webdav/site/ctei/shared/CTEI/working_papers/CTEI-2011-07.pdf.

[79] The Group of 7 (G-7) includes Canada, France, Germany, Italy, Japan, the United States, and the United Kingdom.

[80] The Group of 20 (G-20) includes the G-7 countries plus Argentina, Australia, Brazil, Canada, China, India, Indonesia, Mexico, Russia, Saudi Arabia, South Africa, South Korea, Turkey, and the European Union (EU). For more on the G-20, see CRS Report R40977, *The G-20 and International Economic Cooperation: Background and Implications for Congress*, by Rebecca M. Nelson.

agreed to halt the depreciation of the U.S. dollar through a host of different policy measures, including taxes, public spending, and interest rates. Some economists argue that the Plaza and Louvre Accords were successful because they reinforced economic fundamentals that were pushing exchange rates in the desired direction.

Additionally, small groups of countries have executed coordinated interventions in foreign exchange markets to shape the relative value of currencies. For example, the G-7 countries have coordinated interventions a number of times: in 1995, to halt the dollar's fall against the yen; in 2000, to support the value of the euro after its introduction; and in 2011, to stem appreciation of the yen following a major crisis in Japan.[81] This coordination has occurred on an ad hoc, voluntary basis. It is not based on any specific set of rules or commitments on exchange rates, and has been limited to a small group of advanced economies.

U.S. Law: The 1988 Trade Act

In 1988, Congress enacted the "Exchange Rates and International Economic Policy Coordination Act of 1988" as part of the Omnibus Trade and Competitiveness Act of 1988 (the 1988 Trade Act),[82] when many policy makers were concerned about the appreciation of the U.S. dollar and large U.S. trade deficits.[83] A key component of this act requires the Treasury Department to analyze on an annual basis the exchange rate policies of foreign countries, in consultation with the IMF, and "consider whether countries manipulate the rate of exchange between their currency and the United States dollar for purposes of preventing effective balance of payments adjustments or gaining unfair competitive advantage in international trade." If "manipulation" is occurring with respect to countries that have (1) global currency account surpluses and (2) significant bilateral trade surpluses with the United States, the Secretary of the Treasury is to initiate negotiations, through the IMF or bilaterally, to ensure adjustment in the exchange rate and eliminate the "unfair" trade advantage. The Secretary of the Treasury is not required to start negotiations in cases where they would have a serious detrimental impact on vital U.S. economic and security interests.

Additionally, the act requires the Treasury Secretary to submit a report annually to the Senate and House Banking Committees, on or before October 15, with written six-month updates (on April 15), and the Secretary is expected to testify on the reports as requested.[84] The reports are to address a host of issues related to exchange rate policies, such as currency market developments; currency interventions undertaken to adjust the exchange rate of the dollar; the impact of the exchange rate on U.S. competitiveness; and the outcomes of Treasury negotiations on currency issues, among others.

Since the 1988 Trade Act was enacted, the Treasury Department has identified three countries as manipulating their currencies under the Trade Act's terms: China, Taiwan, and South Korea.[85]

---

[81] "Divine Intervention," *Economist*, March 27, 2008.

[82] P.L. 100-418; 22 U.S.C. 5301-5306.

[83] C. Randall Henning, "Congress, Treasury, and the Accountability of Exchange Rate Policy: How the 1988 Trade Act Should be Reformed," Institute for International Economics Working Paper 07-8, September 2007, http://www.iie.com/publications/wp/wp07-8.pdf.

[84] The Treasury Department also posts the currency reports on its website: http://www.treasury.gov/resource-center/international/exchange-rate-policies/Pages/index.aspx.

[85] Treasury cited Taiwan and South Korea in 1988 and China in 1992. Taiwan's and South Korea's citations lasted for (continued...)

These designations occurred in the late 1980s and early 1990s; Treasury has not found currency manipulation under the terms of the 1988 Trade Act since it last cited China in 1994. Some Members of Congress have been concerned by what they perceive as inaction by the Treasury Department on currency manipulation. In 2004, Congress passed legislation asking the Treasury Secretary to submit a report "describing how statutory provisions addressing currency manipulation by America's trading partners ... can be better clarified administratively to provide for improved and more predictable evaluation, and to enable the problem of currency manipulation to be better understood by the American people."[86] In 2005, the Government Accountability Office (GAO) completed a study on Treasury's assessments of whether countries manipulate their currencies for trade advantage.[87] One conclusion in the report was that "Treasury has generally complied with the reporting requirements for its exchange rate reports, although its discussion of U.S. economic impacts has become less specific over time."

Trade Promotion Authority and Trade Agreements

Given the potential links between exchange rate policies of other countries and the competitiveness of U.S. industry and exports, Congress has referenced addressing currency issues in previous TPA authorizations. For example, in the Omnibus Trade and Competitiveness Act of 1988, which granted "fast track" authority (the precursor to TPA) to the President, the President was required, among other things, to submit a report to Congress with supporting information after entering a trade agreement. One part of this report was "describing the efforts made by the President to obtain international exchange rate equilibrium."[88]

Additionally, when TPA was last renewed in 2002, Congress included exchange rate issues as a priority that the Administration should promote. The legislation stipulated that the Administration should "seek to establish consultative mechanisms among parties to trade agreements to examine the trade consequences of significant and unanticipated currency movements and to scrutinize whether a foreign government engaged in a pattern of manipulating its currency to promote a competitive advantage in international trade."[89]

A number of free trade agreements (FTAs) were negotiated under the 2002 version of TPA, with Congress approving implementing legislation for FTAs with Chile, Singapore, Australia, Morocco, the Dominican Republic and the Central American countries (CAFTA-DR), Bahrain, Oman, Peru, Colombia, Panama, and South Korea. It is not clear to what extent currency issues were salient issues in the negotiations or in the final agreements.

(...continued)

at least two 6-month reporting periods, while China's lasted for five 6-month reporting periods. Taiwan was cited again in 1992. U.S. Government Accountability Office, *Treasury Assessments Have Not Found Currency Manipulation, but Concerns about Exchange Rates Continue,* GAO-05-351, April 2005, http://www.gao.gov/assets/250/246061.pdf.

[86] Section 221 of the Consolidated Appropriations Act, 2005 (P.L. 108-447).

[87] U.S. Government Accountability Office, *Treasury Assessments Have Not Found Currency Manipulation, but Concerns about Exchange Rates Continue,* GAO-05-351, April 2005, http://www.gao.gov/assets/250/246061.pdf.

[88] Section 1103(a)(2)(B)(iii) of the Omnibus Trade and Competitiveness Act of 1988 (P.L. 100-418).

[89] Section 2102(c)(12) of the Trade Act of 2002 (P.L. 107-210).

Responses to Current Disagreements

To the extent that there has been a formal multilateral response to current disagreements over exchange rates, it has been through discussions at G-7 and G-20 meetings. During meetings in February 2013, for example, the G-7 nations reaffirmed their "long-standing commitment to market-determined exchange rates" and to "not target exchange rates."[90] The G-20 countries pledged to "refrain from competitive devaluation" in February 2013,[91] and more recently in September 2013, that central banks "have committed that future changes to monetary policy settings will continue to be carefully calibrated and clearly communicated."[92] G-7 and G-20 commitments are non-binding, although other enforcement mechanisms, including peer pressure, have been used to ensure compliance in the past.

Current disagreements over exchange rates have not resulted in the IMF or the Treasury Department labeling any countries as currency manipulators, and no country has filed a dispute over exchange rate policies at the WTO. Starting in 2011, Brazil did present three papers on exchange rates and the role of the WTO for discussion at the WTO Working Group on Trade, Debt, and Finance. Reportedly, many other WTO members have approached the discussions with "reserve and skepticism" and believed that the IMF would be the appropriate forum for such a discussion.[93]

Some analysts and policy makers have been concerned that current disagreements have not resulted in more formal action, particularly by the IMF and the Treasury Department, which have the clearest rules pertaining to currency manipulation. They argue that currency manipulation has occurred, but the current frameworks are ineffective at dealing with it. For example, they argue that it is hard to demonstrate that exchange rate policies have been for the express purpose of increasing net exports; the IMF does not have a clear enforcement mechanism for its rules on exchange rates; and the Treasury Department fears retaliation from countries it unilaterally labels as "manipulators." One policy expert has stated that the greatest flaw in the international financial architecture is its failure to effectively counter and deter competitive currency policies.[94]

Other analysts and policy makers contend that the current frameworks on "currency manipulation" are effective. They argue that formal action by the IMF and the Treasury Department has not occurred because countries have not engaged in policies that violate international commitments on exchange rates or triggered U.S. laws pertaining to currency manipulation. Some analysts also believe that the Treasury Department has at various times urged

---

[90] Bank of England; News Release – G7 Statement, February 12, 2013, http://www.bankofengland.co.uk/publications/Pages/news/2013/027.aspx.

[91] Charles Clover, Robin Harding, and Alice Ross, "G20 Agrees to Avoid Currency Wars," *Financial Times*, February 17, 2013; G-20 Communiqué, Meeting of Finance Ministers and Central Bank Governors, Moscow, February 15-16, 2013, available at http://www.g20.org/documents/.

[92] G-20 Leaders' Declaration, September 2013, St. Petersburg, http://www.g20.org/documents.

[93] Vera Thorstensen, Daniel Ramos, and Caronlina Muller, "The 'Missing Link' Between the WTO and IMF," *Journal of International Economic Law*, vol. 16, no. 2 (2013), pp. 353-381.

[94] Fred Bergsten, "Currency Wars, the Economy of the United States, and Reform of the International Monetary System," Remarks at Peterson Institute for International Economics, May 16, 2013, http://www.iie.com/publications/papers/bergsten201305.pdf.

---

countries to address exchange rate issues behind-the-scenes, even if it has not publicly labeled any countries as currency manipulators in recent years.[95]

Policy Options for Congress

Some Members of Congress have proposed taking action on currency issues, because they are concerned about the impact of other countries' exchange rate policies on the competitiveness of U.S. exports and import-competing firms. Some Members could also be concerned that other countries have accused the United States of engaging in "currency wars." If Members did decide to take action on exchange rates, there are a number of options for doing so, some of which Members are already pursuing. Policy options could include, among others:

(1) Maintaining the status quo: Even though Members may be concerned about supporting U.S. exports and jobs from "unfair" exchange rate policies adopted by other countries, there may be a number of reasons to refrain from taking action on exchange rate disputes:

- There is much debate among economists on how to calculate a currency's "equilibrium" or "fundamental" long-term value, making the classification of currencies as undervalued or overvalued complex and subject to much discussion, with different models at times yielding very different results. Some economists also believe that currency interventions have limited, short-term effects, particularly on floating currencies, given the high volumes of capital flows.

- U.S. imports from trading partners with weak currencies are less expensive than they would be otherwise. Lower-cost imports may benefit U.S. businesses that purchase inputs from abroad and U.S. consumers.

- Unilaterally labeling a country as a currency manipulator or leading a multilateral charge against currency manipulation could trigger retaliation by other countries. For example, the United States has a low savings rate and benefits from low interest rates. Countries labeled as currency "manipulators" could buy fewer U.S. government bonds, making it more expensive and potentially harder for the U.S. government to finance its budget deficit.

- Tensions over exchange rates could dissipate as the global economy strengthens, particularly if developed economies end quantitative easing. For example, Brazil's concerns about the real appreciating against the U.S. dollar have reversed in recent months (and now Brazil is concerned about the real depreciating against the U.S. dollar too much).

(2) Urging the Administration to address currency disputes at the IMF or WTO: Addressing currency disputes in formal international institutions may provide broad, multilateral support for decisions that are reached. The IMF and the WTO have been the international institutions identified as best suited for dealing with exchange rate disputes, because the IMF has the clearest set of commitments relating to currency manipulation, and the WTO is unique among international financial institutions in that it has a clear enforcement mechanism. However,

---

[95] For example, see Annie Lowrey, "A Tightrope on China's Currency," *New York Times*, October 22, 2012.

addressing disputes over exchange rates at the IMF and WTO may run into obstacles. For example, the IMF Executive Board may find it too politically sensitive to label a country as a "currency manipulator." Congress could ask the Administration to push for changes to IMF and/or WTO rules to allow currency disputes to be addressed more clearly under these organizations, but this could be a complicated process that requires multilateral consensus.

(3) Urging the Administration to strengthen informal international cooperation on exchange rates: For example, Congress could urge the Treasury Department to continue its push for G-20 commitments on (1) greater transparency of foreign reserve data and currency intervention operations; and (2) avoidance of official public statements intended to influence exchange rate levels.[96] Additionally, Congress could also urge the Administration to push for informal agreements to re-align the value of currencies, similar to the Plaza Accord and the Louvre Accord in the 1980s. However, some question whether informal cooperation can effectively foster cooperation on exchange rates consistently, not just on an as-needed or ad-hoc basis. The G-7 excludes large emerging market economies that are major players in the global economy, but, at the same time, the G-20 may be too large and heterogeneous to reach meaningful agreements. Also, since agreements reached at the G-7 and G-20 are non-binding, questions have been raised about the effectiveness of these forums. This approach would also be unlikely to address manipulation by countries outside the G-7 or G-20, although some argue that G-20 action in particular would involve the major economies in the international economy.

(4) Addressing currency issues in trade agreements or as a negotiating objective in TPA: Congress could address concerns about the exchange rate policies of other countries by urging the Administration to address currency issues in the free trade agreements currently under negotiation, including the TPP and TTIP. For example, Representative Levin released a proposal to address currency manipulation in the TPP in July 2013.[97] With regards to any legislation renewing TPA, Congress could also identify currency issues as a trade policy priority, similar to the provisions included in the 2002 TPA legislation, or include currency issues as a more formal trade negotiating objective.

Seeking to include currency issues in a trade agreement could make the agreement more difficult to conclude. There are also different views about how currency issues could or should be addressed. Some have called for enforceable provisions, but there may be disagreement over how exchange rate disputes would be adjudicated. Others have called for cooperative frameworks to examine currency issues. Additionally, any negotiated agreement on currency disagreements would be limited in scope, because it would apply to negotiating parties to the agreement and not to countries in the global economy more broadly.

(5) Passing new legislation on undervalued exchange rates or amending existing legislation on currency manipulation: Some argue that legislation could directly address the concerns of

---

[96] U.S. Department of the Treasury, Office of International Affairs, "Report to Congress on International Economic and Exchange Rate Policies," April 12, 2013, http://www.treasury.gov/resource-center/international/exchange-rate-policies/Documents/Foreign%20Exchange%20Report%20April%202013.pdf.

[97] U.S. Representative Sander Levin, "U.S.-Japan Automotive Trade: Proposal to Level the Playing Field," http://www.piie.com/publications/papers/levin20130723proposal.pdf. The proposal calls for, among other things, a commitment by TPP countries to avoid manipulating exchange rates to gain an unfair competitive advantage over other TPP countries; establishing specific benchmarks by which to determine whether a TPP country has manipulated its exchange rate; and enforcing commitments to avoid exchange rate manipulation through the normal dispute settlement mechanism of the TPP agreement.

---

certain U.S. exporters and import-sensitive producers about "unfair" exchange rate policies of other countries, and could provide U.S. exporters with recourse and/or encourage other countries to push up the value of their currencies. Additionally, a possible advantage of legislation relating to countries with "undervalued" or "misaligned" currencies is that it could apply to all countries, not just a subset of countries, such as countries that are party to a trade negotiation with the United States.

Several pieces of legislation on exchange rates have been introduced in previous Congresses, and two bills have been introduced in the 113th Congress:

- **The Currency Reform for Fair Trade Act (H.R. 1276)** would affect the treatment of imports from countries with fundamentally undervalued exchange rates. If passed, it would broaden the definition of a "countervailable" subsidy (or a subsidy that could be eligible to be offset through higher import duties) to include the benefit conferred on merchandise imports into the United States from foreign countries with fundamentally undervalued currencies.[98]

- **The Currency Exchange Rate Oversight Reform Act of 2013 (S. 1114)** proposes methods for addressing exchange rate issues. Among other provisions, the legislation prescribes negotiations and consultations with countries with fundamentally misaligned exchange rates, and actions to take against "priority action" countries that have failed, or persistently failed, to take action to eliminate exchange rate misalignments.[99]

Others argue that it could be difficult to reach consensus on if, and if so, by how much, a currency is undervalued or misaligned. Additionally, if currency "manipulation" was defined in statute, it could be inflexible. As mentioned earlier, unilateral legislation could also provoke countries that are labeled as having undervalued currencies, and cause them to retaliate in ways that undermine other U.S. interests. Legislation could also harm U.S. producers and consumers that buy and use imported goods. Finally, some have raised questions about whether legislation relating to import duties would violate WTO rules.

---

[98] The bill provides details on how it would be determined if a country had a fundamentally undervalued currency, and the size of the real effective exchange rate undervaluation. Introduced by Representative Levin, it is similar to bills introduced by Representative Levin in the 112th Congress (H.R. 639) and in the 111th Congress (H.R. 2378). The House passed H.R. 2378 in September 2010.

[99] More generally, the bill requires the Treasury Department to issue a semiannual report to Congress on international monetary policy and exchange rates; prescribes negotiations and consultations with countries with fundamentally misaligned exchange rates, and actions to take against "priority action" countries that have failed, or persistently failed, to take action to eliminate the fundamental exchange rate misalignment; requires the Treasury Secretary to oppose any proposed changes in the international financial institutions that would increase the representation of countries with fundamentally misaligned currencies that are designated for priority action; amends countervailing and antidumping duty legislation to incorporate imports from countries with fundamentally misaligned currencies; and establishes an Advisory Committee on International Exchange Rate Policy. It would also repeal the Exchange Rates and International Economic Policy Coordination Act of 1988. Introduced by Senator Brown, this bill is similar to S. 1619, which Senator Brown introduced in the 112th Congress and was passed by the Senate in October 2011.

Conclusion

Exchange rates are important prices in the global economy, and changes in exchange rates have potentially substantial implications for international trade and investment flows across countries. Following the global financial crisis of 2008-2009, tensions among countries over exchange rate policies have arguably broadened. Some policy makers and analysts have expressed concerns that some governments are pursuing exchange rate policies to gain a trade advantage, as many countries grapple with economic recession or slow growth and high unemployment following the financial crisis. Concerns have focused on both government interventions in currency markets in a number of other countries, including China and Switzerland, and expansionary monetary policies in some developed economies. On the other hand, some economists argue that the effects of exchange rate policies are nuanced, creating winners and losers, and that it is hard to make generalized claims about the negative effects of "currency wars."

Members concerned about the competitiveness of the United States may want to weigh the pros and cons of taking action on exchange rate disputes. If policy makers do want to take action, a number of policy options are available. Some Members of Congress have proposed legislation to address currency undervaluation by other countries and proposed addressing currency issues in on-going trade negotiations, particularly in the context of the proposed TPP and any renewal of TPA. Members could also urge the Administration to press the issue more forcefully at international institutions, such as the IMF or WTO, or more informal forums for international cooperation, including the G-7 or the G-20.

To date, the most formal response to current tensions over exchange rates has been through discussions at G-7 and G-20 meetings. Although frameworks have been set up for addressing currency "manipulation" at the IMF and through U.S. law, neither the IMF nor the U.S. Treasury Department has taken formal action on current disputes over exchange rates. There are debates about why formal action has not been taken at these institutions. One general complicating factor in addressing currency disputes is that estimating a currency's "fundamental" or "true" value is extremely complex and subject to debate among economists.

Author Contact Information

Rebecca M. Nelson
Analyst in International Trade and Finance
rnelson@crs.loc.gov, 7-6819

Acknowledgments

Hannah Fisher and Amber Wilhelm provided assistance with the figures for this report.

www.ingramcontent.com/pod-product-compliance
Lightning Source LLC
Chambersburg PA
CBHW080736290526

45790CB00008B/3222